Laura Merz and Aino Järvinen

1,001 CREATURES

Translated from the Finnish
by Emily Jeremiah

Restless Books
Brooklyn, New York

First published as *Tuhat ja yksi otusta* by Etana Editions, Helsinki, 2016
English edition published in agreement with the Koja Agency.

This book is made possible by the New York State Council on the Arts
with the support of Governor Andrew M. Cuomo and the New York State Legislature.

This book is supported in part by an award from the National Endowment for the Arts.

This work has been published with the financial assistance of
FILI – Finnish Literature Exchange

First Restless Books hardcover edition September 2020

Hardcover ISBN: 9781632062680
Library of Congress Control Number: 2019944177

Cover design by Jonathan Yamakami
Cover illustration by Laura Merz

Printed in Italy

1 3 5 7 9 10 8 6 4 2

Restless Books, Inc.
232 3rd Street, Suite A101
Brooklyn, NY 11215

www.restlessbooks.org
publisher@restlessbooks.org

CONTENTS

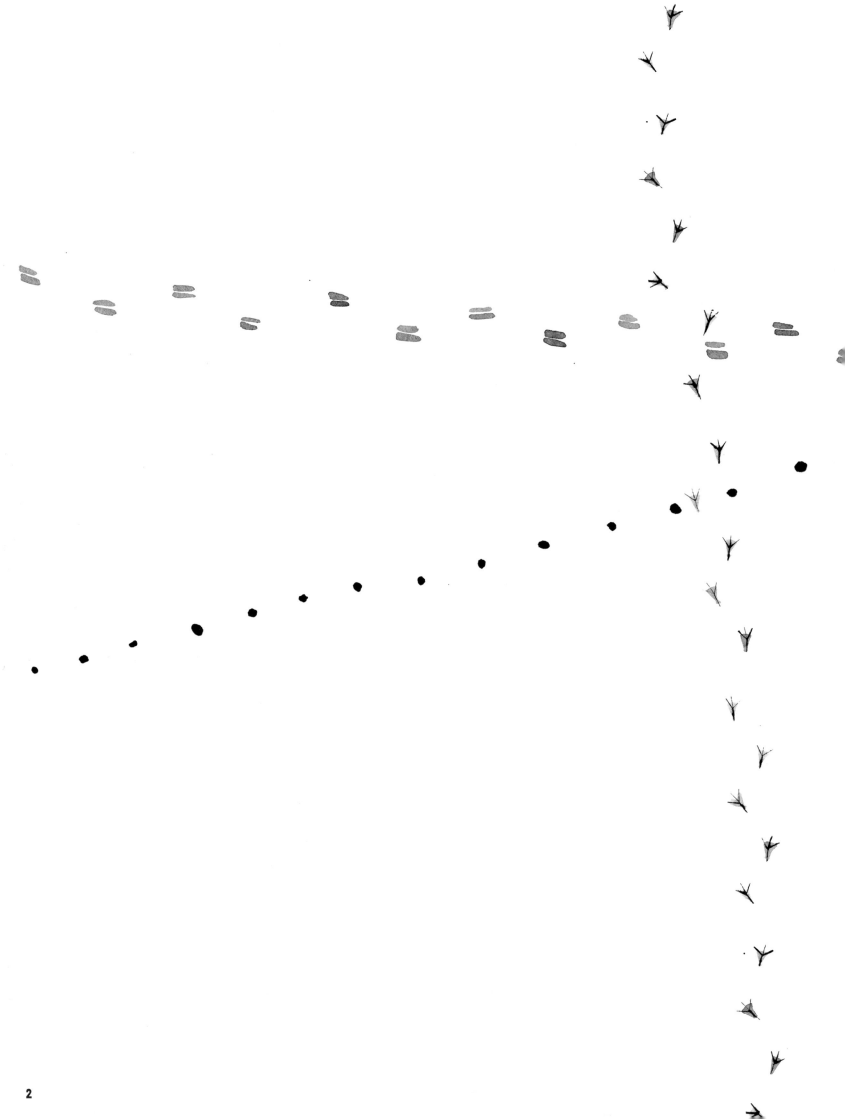

Our globe teems with creatures great and small.
The ground is trampled on by paws, claws, hooves, flippers . . . .
What creatures have been here?

TRUMPET OF THE JUNGLE

A thudding on the field.
Here comes the multipurpose marvel of the jungle,
Elephant and TRUNK!

Trunk sniffs the air.
Trunk sinks to the ground and digs.

Trunk reaches out to a tree, grabs hold of leaves,
gobbles them up.
Chomp!
Trunk dives into the river, guzzles up water
and sprays it into her mouth.
No more thirst!

Trunk gently caresses the little elephant's side.

If you get too close, the trunk will blow like a horn.
If you don't believe the warning, the trunk will knock
you over!

Can you mimic the trumpeting sound of the elephant's
trunk?

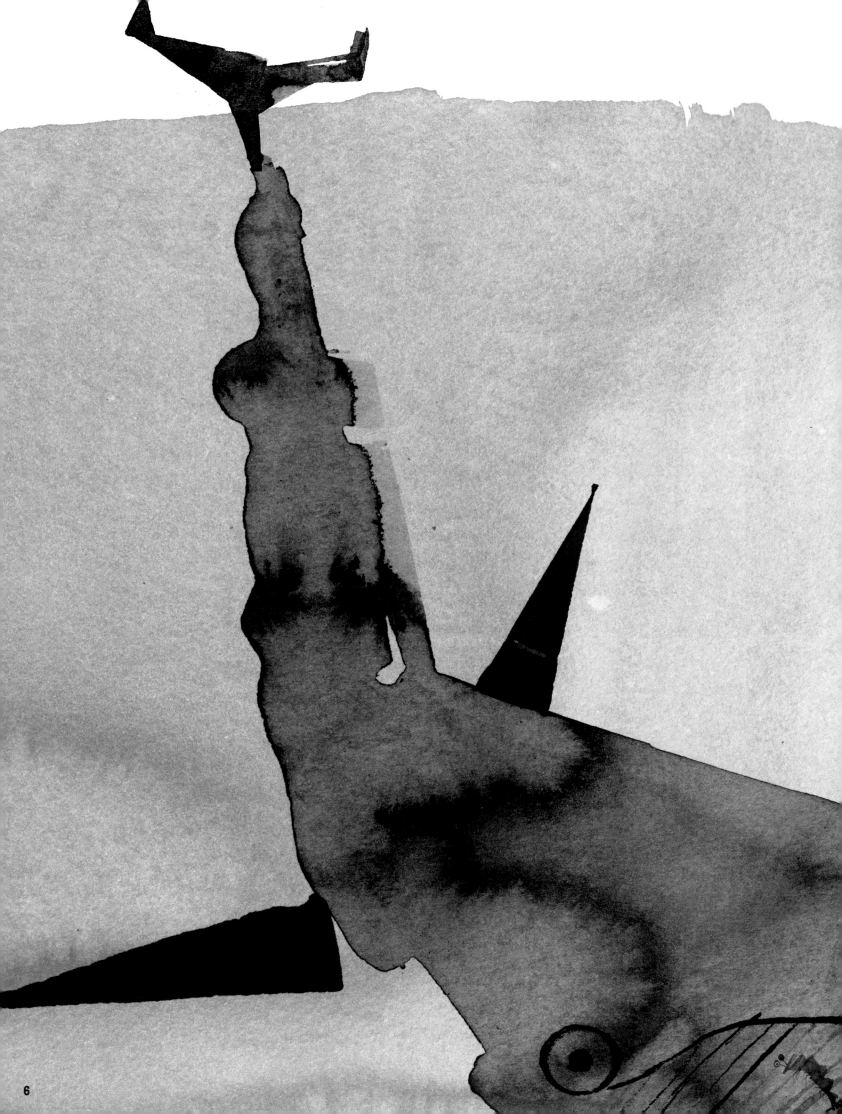

GIANT OF THE SEAS

The blue whale is the world's largest creature.

Could it really be bigger than an elephant?
Oh yes, a blue whale's tongue weighs as
much as a whole elephant!

What does this giant eat?
It probably gobbles up the biggest fish in the sea!

On the contrary!
The food of the blue whale is a tiny crustacean called krill.

Mouth open, the whale dives into the swarm of krill
and sifts out water.
In order to do that it has baleen, instead of teeth.
It swims and eats, eats and swims.
A million krill is just the start!

Occasionally, a beautiful plume of mist rises up from the sea.
The blue whale put it there.
Do you know how or why?

A MASTER OF DISGUISE

Inside an octopus beat three hearts.
What a special creature!

On a bed of sand – it looks like sand.
On a mound of stones – it is a stone.
It changes the color and texture of its skin according
to its surroundings.

Soon it won't be visible at all.
A huge cloud of ink spreads out in the sea.
Inside it, the octopus is well hidden.
The enemy can't attack the master of disguise now!

Can you use the octopus's tricks when you're playing
hide-and-seek?

A SLIMY JELLY FLOWER

The sea covers more than half the surface of the earth.
Strange creatures dwell in its depths
which we can't even imagine.

One of the most unusual is the jellyfish.
Floating in the sea, it looks like a beautiful flower,
but on the beach, it's just a heap of slimy jelly.

Jellyfish don't have bones, brains, or hearts.
Still they hunt down their food.
Some jellyfish are poisonous and deadly.
Some can carry on with their lives
even if they're cut in two!
Some shine like lanterns in the dark sea.

The deeper you go,
the stranger the animals you'll find.

Is that even an animal, or is it a plant?
Can you think up a name for such a creature?

CAN YOU DIG IT?

Things go on underground!
Mud, sand, crevices between stones –
they teem with worms, millipedes,
woodlice, and all sorts of other
creepy-crawlies.

The mole feasts on them,
that little mammal that lives
completely underground.

The mole doesn't navigate by sight
or sound, neither sees nor hears.
It's hard to use either sense underground!
With its strong, spade-like front paws
this creature digs tunnels and seeks food.

Wow, fifteen feet in an hour! Now it's time to rest.
The mole takes a nap. Then it digs again.
It takes another nap, then digs again.
Night or day, it makes no difference.

There is a new heap of earth
in the morning, in the middle of the yard.
Where did that come from?

TWILIGHT FLIER

Here's a strange creature!
Like a mouse, but with leathery wings.
And it hangs, head down, in the hollow of a tree all day.

Come twilight, the creature wakes, comes out of hiding.
It's a bat!
It flits wildly with its large wings, here and there,
and snaps up insects for food.

How come it doesn't crash into anything, even though
it's dark?

The bat emits high-pitched sounds while flying
which we can't hear.
The creature itself hears the echo with its large ears.
The echo steers its flight,
so it finds its prey and avoids crashes.

Have you noticed that in the dark,
ears are more important than eyes?

HIDE-AND-SEEK

Teddy, honey-paw, king of the forest:
the bear has many nicknames.

Could you meet the king of the forest while out looking for mushrooms?
Hardly.
Long before you see a bear
it'll have sniffed you out and retreated deep into the trees.

You'll only find traces.
Who's destroyed the anthill?

This large creature loves small delicacies!
The bear combs through the ant hill with its big paws
and pops the occupants into its mouth.
The hardworking ants don't take a break.
In the wake of the destruction, they quickly repair their hill
and get on with their work.

What if the bear fancies honey?
Is the beehive easy prey?

A HOWLING IN THE NIGHT

A wolf cub is born into a huge family
headed up by its own mother and father.
It's safe to romp near the lair
when your older siblings are babysitting.

Looking for food involves skillful cooperation for a pack of wolves;
each wolf has its task
and the prey is shared among them all.

When the howl of the wolves rings out in the wilderness at night,
all of nature falls silent, to listen.
The wolves are calling to each other:
a hunting trip is about to begin.

The cub stays in the lair, sleeping.
When will it get to go along too?

FOOD! FOOD!

Father owl sits on the branch as evening falls.
It's time to go hunting.

Mother owl stays in the nest
keeping her newly hatched owlets warm.
Father owl will have to feed the whole family on his own!
Quite a job!

The owl's head can swivel nearly all the way round
to help it spot its prey with those sharp eyes.
Its sensitive ears pick up a scratching sound in the grass.
Thanks to its soft feathers, the attack is completely silent.
The sharp claws strike in a single second!

A hungry cheeping comes from the nest.
The owlet swallows the mouse with one gulp.
More!

When will father owl have time to sleep?

KING OF THE ICE

Would you ever guess that the polar bear's skin is pitch-black
and the fur transparent?
Colors really are the reflection of light.
In the sunshine against all the bright, white snow,
the polar bear is a white, fluffy giant.

The camouflage works well.
The unsuspecting seal doesn't notice
the white creature in the middle of the white landscape.
Soon the bear will eat his favorite treat.

The king of the ice needs icy surroundings,
and seal hunting only works on ice.

What will the bear eat if the ice melts?

A ROCKY PROPOSAL

Adélie penguins build their nests using small stones.
Searching for stones in a landscape of ice and snow
is hard work!

The male penguin charms his spouse with his stock of stones.
The couples build their nests together,
but the female penguin has her doubts.

Perhaps it's not advisable to reject other suitors just yet . . .
What if the spouse doesn't return from his hunting trip?

Again, a new gift changes owners,
bustling among the penguin community.
Some nests are even looted!
Stones clink like little coins.

Why is the nest made of stones, and not snow?

WATER DANCERS

The sea lion has lounged around enough.
It's time to get back to the sea.
Fifteen feet: oh, what a long journey.
In the end it manages to flop clumsily to the water's edge.

Splash! No trace of clumsiness!
The sea lion dives down into the depths, dozens of yards.
It races up to the surface, jumps high into the air,
despite weighing many hundreds of pounds.
It's a brilliant swimmer,
and sees and hears acutely underwater.

Baby sea lions are born on land,
but after only a couple of weeks, the pups too decide to test the water.
Soon they are swimming and diving like their parents.

How can one become a master so quickly?

27

ONWARD AND UPWARD!

Migratory birds are brilliant navigators!
They look down at the land from above as if it were a large map.
They follow mountain ranges, rivers, lakes, and shorelines.
The sun, the moon, and the stars act as signposts along the route.

But why do birds make such a long passage every year?

The reason is clear: the long, bright nights in the north.
In the south it's warm, but the nights are long and dark.
Up in the north there's enough grub for the chicks.
Insects buzz in the air from early in the morning until late at night.
That's why the north is the best place to build a nest!

The light lessens in autumn.
Then it's time to move south, away from the cold, dark winter.

Surely we'll meet again next spring?

SHIP OF THE DESERT

The camel has a special way of walking.
It puts two feet from the same side onto the ground at once,
alternating right then left.
That's why it rocks like a boat on the waves.

The camel carries people and things through the hot, sandy desert,
which is as boundless as the open sea.
There's no better assistant for a human than the ship of the desert!

It has its own specialist equipment:
The hump is like the camel's lunch box, full of fat,
so the creature can go for days without eating or drinking.

The eyes and the nose are special.
Thick lashes and heavy lids protect the eyes in a sandstorm.
If there's lots of dust around, the camel can close its nostrils.
And then it's off again!

Have you tried walking like a camel?

WORLD'S FASTEST RUNNER

While other felines tread with soft paws,
the cheetah's claws are always half out.
Its secret, the sprinter's gear . . . spikes!

When the spikes stick into the ground, the cheetah gets a head start.
It gets up to full speed in seconds.
The cheetah's long tail helps it maintain balance during quick turns.

This cat has no rivals in a race.
The chase is over in an instant.

Thanks to its camouflage, the cheetah can blend into the landscape.
Can you find others hiding in the picture?

JUNGLE'S
LONELY HUNTER

The tiger is the world's biggest cat.
Just as you are recognized by your face,
the tiger can be identified by its stripes.
No two tigers in the world have the same stripes.

Its camouflage helps it hide in the shadows of the jungle.
But it's still not always easy to find food.
Patience is required.

The hungry tiger hides in the foliage.
It listens.
Branches crack, leaves rustle.
The tiger waits, waits, waits.
Finally it pounces!
But no! Again the nimble creature escapes.

Finally, success for the lone wanderer.
It eats slowly and rests for many days.

When the predator succeeds, its prey is eaten.
But when the prey manages to escape,
how will the predator survive?

COOPERATIVE MEALTIMES

Standing in the wetland,
the water buffalo's coat crawls with ticks!
The insects make life uncomfortable.
So annoying!

Will there be no peace in which to eat?

A heron flies over.
Watch: it lands on the back of the large creature.
The water buffalo isn't disturbed;
on the contrary.

The heron begins its meal.
Ticks and other insects, yummy!
It rids the buffalo's coat of the pesky bugs.

The buffalo is relieved.
It gulps down grass
and enjoys the scratching.

But is it nice for the heron to eat on a moving table?

A BRAVE DENTIST

The large crocodile has climbed the banks of the river to rest.
All the animals know to beware of this frightening creature.

But now what's happening?
A bird flies over; it's called a crocodile bird.
It steps straight inside the reptile's open jaws!
Help, what's going on here?!

Nothing bad, both of them know.
The dentist is welcome.
The crocodile waits, satisfied,
as the bird cleans its teeth, getting into all the nooks and crannies.

The winged creature eats an excellent meal of insects and scraps of food.
The beast lets it eat in peace.

Where does the bird get such courage from?

OUR CLEVER RELATIVES

A small river interrupts the gorilla's wanderings in the jungle.
The creature breaks off a branch to use as a measuring stick.
Let's see if the river can be crossed by wading!

The ape weighs nuts in its hand.
It knows the lighter one is ripe.
Grab a stone, and break the shell with one blow. Yum!

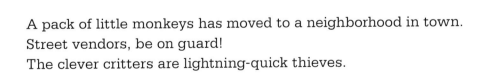

A pack of little monkeys has moved to a neighborhood in town.
Street vendors, be on guard!
The clever critters are lightning-quick thieves.

Apes and monkeys are primates, like us.
The secret of primates is our opposable thumbs.
With their help, we can handle tools.

Try to pick a book up off the floor with one hand . . .
without using your thumb!

QUEEN OF THE PRIDE

The lioness is a proud mother.
She tenderly looks after her newborn cubs,
which stay by her side, blind and helpless.

The father's task is to defend the pack.
His threatening roar can be heard five miles away.

When the cubs grow up,
their mother teaches them the way of lions:
hunting prey and eating meat!

Who is the best hunter of the pack?
Probably the strong male lion, with his handsome mane?
No, females are nimbler and more skillful.
Mom is the best at procuring food.

But where is the male lion, as the female does
all the work?

A FLIGHTLESS BIRD

The ostrich, the world's largest living bird, can't fly.
But it can run,
hurtling at such a speed that in town,
it would get pulled over for speeding.

The ostrich flock is a large family in which work is shared.
The shared nest fills with enormous, thick-shelled eggs.
The flock's head couple is tasked with hatching them in turn.

When the chick is ready to come out,
it knocks at the shell for up to half a day before it breaks out.
Its mother is there!

How does the mother know her chick from all the others?

A FEISTY HERBIVORE

The bushes rustle
as the rhino drives the intruder away.
Did it look that dangerous?

Perhaps not, but the rhino with poor eyesight
has a great deal of bravery.
This creature won't stand for any disruption!
Using its handsome horn as a weapon, the rhino will go up against anyone.

Usually, this wild-looking creature leads quite a peaceful life.
It eats grass, and digs in the dirt with its horn
for roots to eat.
At the same time, it spreads plant seeds all around.

It's good for plants when animals churn up the mud.
Look, that little clump of grass is growing there
because the rhino was here!

What did the rhino get angry about this time?

ZEALOUS ESCAPE ARTISTS

How does a zebra recognize its mother?
By her stripes, of course!

No one else can make head or tail of them.
When the zeal of zebras sprints off to escape,
the stalking predator sees only a black-and-white blur.
No heads or tails!
What to seize onto?

Insects marvel too;
the stripes quiver in their eyes.
Where to jab your stinger?

There are many kinds of camouflage.
The zebra, the cheerful stripy-pants of the savannah,
must be pleased with its own.

Does the zebra's camouflage only work in a zeal?

A GREAT VIEW

The giraffe munches in peace on juicy leaves
that no other creature can reach.

But having a long neck can be a little tricky.
It's awkward lying down and difficult getting up.
That's why the giraffe prefers to sleep standing up.
It just takes little naps now and then,
getting on splendidly that way.

Bending down toward water requires balance;
otherwise the whole creature will collapse like a crooked crane.
Luckily the giraffe isn't thirsty very often.
The juicy leaves up high are full of water.

While chewing away, the world's tallest creature
looks nobly across the savannah.

Now something has thudded onto the ground from more than seven feet up!
What is it?

A STINKY WARNING

On the surface you can see only eyes, nostrils, and small ears,
but under the water there is something gigantic.
The hippo lounges in the river all day.
It can't bear to be in the heat of the sun.

Come evening, the creature trundles onto land.
For many hours during the night, it crunches away at its vegetarian food.
It looks like a restful task,
but when the hippo gets angry, it becomes wild.
Don't get in its way!

The hippo pees and poops at the same time,
turning its tail like a propeller.
Spraying everywhere. Yuck, disgusting!

Or is that its way of keeping intruders away?

A SMELLY BUT VERY IMPORTANT JOB

You can say it straight:
the dung beetle eats poop.
Don't laugh! Dung beetles have an important task.

Without the work of beetles, the savannah would be covered in dung.
The hardworking creatures break down animal droppings
and turn them into nutrients.

So the plants fare well,
as do the animals that eat plants,
which are themselves food for predators.
In nature, everything affects everything else.

When the dung beetle rolls up the dung into balls
and takes it to its hiding place,
it uses the Milky Way to navigate.

The poop-eating beetle looks to the stars!
The cycle of nature is clear
in this funny little miracle.

Under the sun, the moon, and the stars
all the creatures of the world, big and small,
carry out their own tasks
as part of nature's great balance.

But one of the creatures is more curious than the others.
Its name is "human."

It stops and it thinks.
It marvels and it investigates.

It makes up a story.
It draws a picture.

What's in the picture?

About the Illustrator:

Laura Merz is a visual artist, illustrator, and textile designer from Finland specializing in experimental drawing, wildlife-themed works and children's culture. Her works have been shown in solo and group exhibitions both in Finland and around the world. Laura is the illustrator of two award-winning children's books, and she teaches art workshops to children with a refugee background in partnership with the Berlin-based NGO Pass the Crayon and the Finnish organization All Our Children.

About the Author:

Aino Järvinen is a retired teacher of Finnish language and literature. Aino loves writing and collaborates with her goddaughter and visual artist Laura Merz on children's books based on Laura's unique animal drawings. Aino has seen Laura grow from an animal-loving little girl into a fantastic artist whose works are based on an endless interest in nature.

Laura Merz and Aino Järvinen's debut book, *1,001 Creatures*, received The Most Beautiful Books of 2016 prize, which is awarded by the Finnish Book Art Committee.

About the Translator:

Emily Jeremiah was born in Kent in 1975, and now lives in London. A professor at Royal Holloway, University of London, she is the author of three academic books. She is also an award-winning translator of poetry and fiction. With her Finnish mother Fleur Jeremiah, she has co-translated four novels for Peirene Press, and she has published two selections of poetry, by Eeva-Liisa Manner and Sirkka Turkka, with Waterloo Press. She has two novellas forthcoming: Blue Moments (Valley Press, 2020) and An Approach to Black (Reflex Press, 2021).